MW01618234
de
ANTINE
Cléopatre
Gazelle

THE SHOPPING BAG

PORTABLE ART

FARMERS' MARKET '85

1982
BRITAIN
THEN & NOW
NEIMAN·MARCUS FORTNIGHT XXVIII
OCTOBER 15TH · NOVEMBER 3RD · 1984

Marshall Field's
& Christmas

THE SHOPPING BAG

PORTABLE ART

by Stephen C. Wagner & Michael L. Closen

DESIGN BY GEORGE CORSILLO

CROWN PUBLISHERS, INC./NEW YORK

Published by Crown Publishers, Inc., 225 Park Avenue South, New York, New York 10003 and represented in Canada by the Canadian MANDA Group

CROWN is a trademark of Crown Publishers, Inc.

Manufactured in Japan

Library of Congress Cataloging-in-Publication Data

Closen, Michael L.
The shopping bag.

1. Shopping bags—Collectors and collecting—
United States. 2. Graphic arts—Themes, motives.
I. Wagner, Stephen C. II. Title.
NK8643.3.C56 1986 741.6 85-29956

ISBN 0-517-56177-8

10 9 8 7 6 5 4 3 2 1

First Edition

Contents

Preface

In preparing this book, we chose what is commonly known as the "shopping bag" for our subject matter. We define the shopping bag as a container that generally has extended side gussets, a flat bottom, and a pair of handles. We selected this variety of bag over ordinary, or flat, bags, recognizing that shopping bags tend to display higher-quality graphics.

In our five years of collecting, we have concentrated on paper bags because the crisp texture of paper lends itself to better graphic reproduction than do other bag surfaces. Our collection totals more than eleven hundred paper shopping bags, along with a few hundred bags of plastic and other materials. Since this number exceeds that of the shopping bag collection of the Smithsonian Institution, the Smithsonian has accepted our offer to donate our bags to its permanent collection. Our efforts to collect our bags and prepare this book have been both challenging and rewarding, and we hope you will find it informative, interesting, and exciting.

A pearl necklace forms an eight, and a necktie creates a four, to introduce Bloomingdale's to 1984 on this unique shopping bag.

Introduction

The common shopping bag has over the course of many decades developed into a work of art. Originally intended as a carrier of purchased goods, its uses have gradually been expanded to picnic tote, storage container, beach bag, traveling companion, and easily accessible carrier of innumerable articles. The graphics printed on the shopping bag have gone beyond their function as advertising for products or retail stores. They have become important expressions of contemporary art.

The need for a portable carrier and the need to advertise were nonexistent during the Middle Ages, a time of town fairs and a rural way of life. As social and technological changes evolved, a new consumerism emerged with new requirements. Urbanization, the development of widespread transportation, the new working class, and the accessibility of money shattered the everyday life of self-sufficiency that had existed without much change for centuries. It is hard for us to imagine a time when one could not stroll to a neighborhood shop or rush to a regional shopping mall and come home with handfuls of shopping bags packed with the latest everyday necessities or fashions. But our twentieth-century consumer life-style is grounded in the Middle Ages, when shopping involved a long journey to the nearest town to trade bulk quantities of necessities that would last several months until the next trip.

Until the sixteenth century, buying and trading were done mainly in bulk. There was little need for wrapping or packaging. Purchasers provided their own containers, such as baskets, jugs, or bowls. But as towns and cities grew, goods could be purchased as often as needed. Purchasing bulk quantities was no longer necessary since smaller quantities would last until the next shopping spree. Thus, items such as nuts, grains, buttons, and needles required some type of wrapping or packaging to contain the small quantities now purchased. To wrap them, unsold manuscript pages were most often used.

Bookstores at the time customarily sold manuscripts by the page, binding them upon request when purchased. Pages and manuscripts that failed to sell as reading material were sold to merchants as scraps for wrapping paper. The paper was twisted into a cone and folded up at the bottom. This became the first paper bag. Paper makers discovered that they could use the coarse dregs from the bottom of their vats to make a low-quality wrapping paper.

English paper makers moved from supplying the wrapping paper to making paper bags by hand. Letterpress printing was used so that a shopkeeper could purchase ready-made bags with stock designs.

With the growth of industrialization came the first paper-bag-making machine. However widespread the bag-making machines became, in both America and Europe, bag making by hand still remained economical and versatile well into the twentieth century.

These early bags, flat in design and originating from the twisted cone, evolved into square and oblong shapes. The simple construction consisted of two side seams, or one center seam and one bottom seam. Bags with extended sides or gussets followed, with a center seam and a pasted flat bottom, and evolved into the popular patent bag, square with a block bottom. This design allowed for a large quantity of goods to be carried. These three designs—the flat, gusset, and patent—remain the basic forms of construction of bags today.

The early bag-making machines simply folded and pasted a continuous flat tube from a reel of paper, then cut the tube into a variety of lengths. One end of each bag was pasted by hand. Later machines combined the operations, thus eliminating all hand work. The addition of a pair of handles produced the carrier bag, or shopping bag as we now know it. Various types of handles were used at first: a cord passing through a pair of washers at the mouth of each side of the bag; a cord running the entire length of the bag across the bottom and back up the opposite side, forming loops at the mouth on both sides; or twine pasted between cardboard strips and the interior of the bag's mouth.

As packaging and bags became more widespread, improved methods of printing were called for. To meet this need a process now known as flexography was developed. Flexography provides fast, accurate, and uniform printing, which now includes halftone work.

The preparation of artwork for the flexographic printing of shopping bags must be done carefully and accurately. Consideration must be given to the amount of overlap where colors meet, the effect of one color overlapping another, the types of ink used, and the type of paper to be printed upon. Close cooperation among designers, engravers, plate makers, ink suppliers, and printers is necessary to obtain outstanding printed results. Halftone screens and the recently developed four-color process in flexographic production can now result in clear, crisp photographic images on shopping bags. Thus today's shopping bags are truly sophisticated in design. Readily accessible to the public, these slick bags are often taken for granted. Forgotten are the many changes and developments the shopping bag went through to become this practical object of portable art.

LIFE IS JUST A BAG OF TRICKS!

GRAPHIC ART

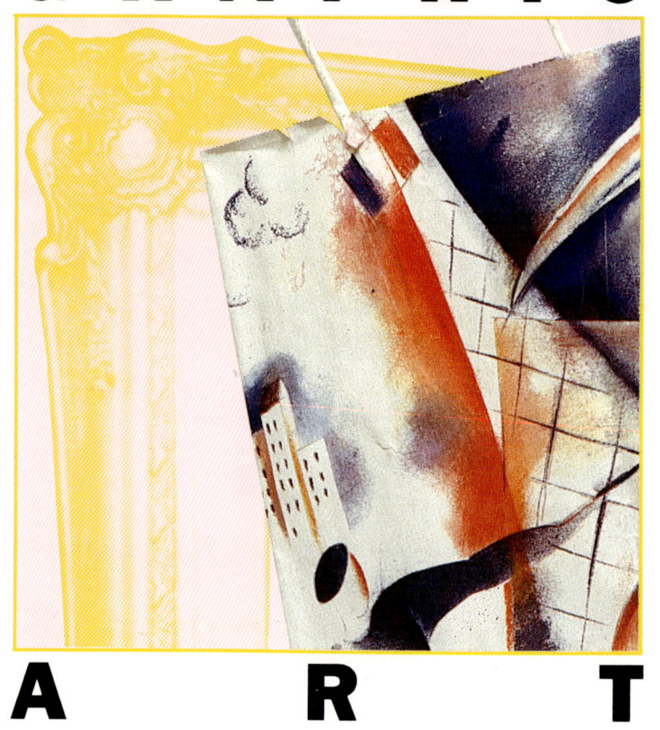

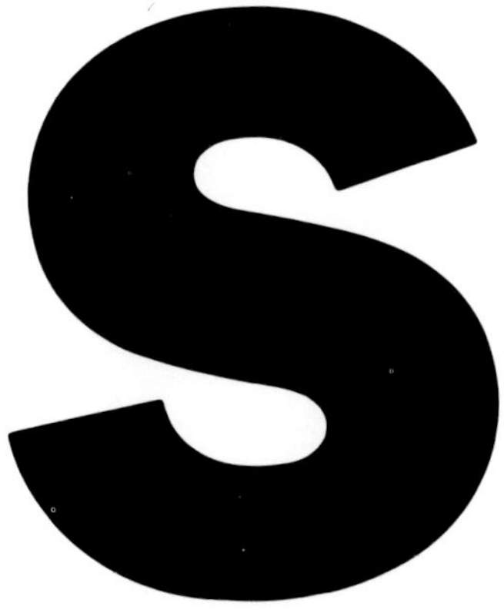idewalks of major cities throughout the world have become kinetic exhibitions of graphic art. Everywhere you look, you see a parade of art of every imaginable subject and style adorning bags carried by shoppers. This widespread display of portable art developed as the result of a number of factors, especially the graphic-arts explosion of the 1960s, when artwork began to appear on everyday items. Matchbooks, greeting cards, record jackets, billboards, and all types of packaging emerged with exciting new graphics, as art became visible to the public to an extent never before seen.

An illustration of this explosion of graphics on shopping bags is the design created for the Neiman-Marcus Fortnight promotion of 1984. The promotion's theme of "Britain—Then and Now" was presented as a nineteenth-century engraving of Queen Elizabeth, shattered by a 1980s new-wave design. This depiction of a revolutionary art style emerging from a traditional form is indicative of what has happened in the art world.

With the advent of more sophisticated printing processes enabling better reproduction of graphics on shopping bags, artists all over the world became attracted to this new medium.

One of the earliest examples of this trend was Andy Warhol's famous soup can. When this piece of art appeared on a shopping bag to promote a pop art exhibit in New York City, it created a sensation. Today this bag is a collector's item.

Erté is another world-famous graphic artist whose work was featured on a shopping bag—the 1982 I. Magnin Christmas bag. Thousands of people who would never have seen his work, were now introduced to his imaginative art. Other prominent artists, such as cartoonists Kliban and Koren, architect Michael Graves, and the contemporary surrealist Nitti, have been commissioned to design shopping bags.

Often stores collaborate with museums or other institutions to create shopping-bag designs, as did Dayton's and the Walker Art Center in Minneapolis. The Art Center commissioned New York abstract artist Frank Stella to design a commemorative shopping bag to publicize the opening of Walker's new galleries in 1984. By helping pay for the bag, Dayton's was able to distribute it throughout its stores.

Sometimes artwork that has been created for other purposes is later printed on shopping bags. For instance, the 1981 Neiman-Marcus Christmas bag displayed an illustration by Disney Studios animator Tom Wood that Walt Disney had once used for his personal Christmas cards. The Disney characters portrayed the joy and festivity of the Christmas season and made a fitting design for the Neiman-Marcus shopping bag.

At other times, the styles of famous artists are mimicked to represent a theme for a seasonal or promotional shopping bag. Burdines in Florida successfully captured the style of a Rousseau tropical scene for its 1978 Christmas bag. And Bloomingdale's has featured allusions to Chagall and Matisse on shopping bags for store promotions.

Reflecting the tastes and trends of society, the shopping bag has been created in diverse styles and designs. During the sixties, bright colors and mod designs highlighted many bags, mirroring the revolutionary culture of the times. As society became more sophisticated and interest in designer products emerged in the seventies, the shopping bag kept in step, with higher-quality designs and a more polished appearance. And as the decade came to a close and the world faced economic difficulties, a return to the traditional and conservative appeared. Bags reflected this in the country look that became so popular in home furnishings and mechandising. With the eighties also came the countercultures of punk rock and new wave. The innovations and colors that emerged from this style account for many bag designs. In 1982, advanced technology in four-color-process printing on shopping bags allowed for designs and effects never before possible, including the use of photography.

Shopping bags are now featured as contemporary still lifes, sculptures, and decorative items. Florida artist Tom Dawkins's oil painting, *Lord & Taylor Shopping Bags with Apples and a Pear*, focuses on the shopping bag as a common item, much as pitchers and basins were used as subject matter in the eighteenth century. Marshall Field's has featured brightly painted shopping bags made of plastic as decorative accents in its contemporary furnishings department.

Shopping bags are now used to make enticing store-window displays. Tiffany's Fifth Avenue store recently caused quite a furor with its window display of a New York bag lady with her crumpled shopping bags stuffed with her belongings seated next to a Park Avenue socialite with her crisp clean bags filled with expensive purchases. People found this true-to-life comparison distasteful and the window was changed prematurely. But not before a photographer had captured it. And it later became a popular New York postcard.

As beauty is in the eye of the beholder, art exists on the sidewalks ready to be noticed and appreciated by the beholder. We need only look and open our minds to enjoy the kinetic display of art that surrounds us. The shopping bag has arrived. It is truly portable art.

The theme "Britain Then and Now" from the 1984 Fortnight promotion inspired Neiman-Marcus in Dallas to create this highly unusual bag design.

These Bloomingdale's shopping bags successfully carry the styles of the famous artists they represent. The allusion to Chagall is from 1983, the allusion to Matisse from 1982.

JOURNAL

Commissioned by I. Magnin, Koren uses his witty and bizarre cartoon style on its 1984 Christmas bag.

Kliban's whimsical talent is evident on the Neiman-Marcus 1981 Christmas shopping bag. Who else would place Santa in a caravan of camels transporting rainbows across the snow?

A woman's hairdo is transformed into a Christmas tree decorated with garlands and lights on the 1982 Christmas shopping bag designed by Erté for I. Magnin.

Christmas in Florida, according to Burdines, may well be like Christmas in a Rousseau tropical painting (1978).

Frank Stella would not consider creating art for a towel or a T-shirt, but the Walker Art Center in Minneapolis was successful in obtaining Stella's consent to have his artwork appear on a shopping bag in 1984.

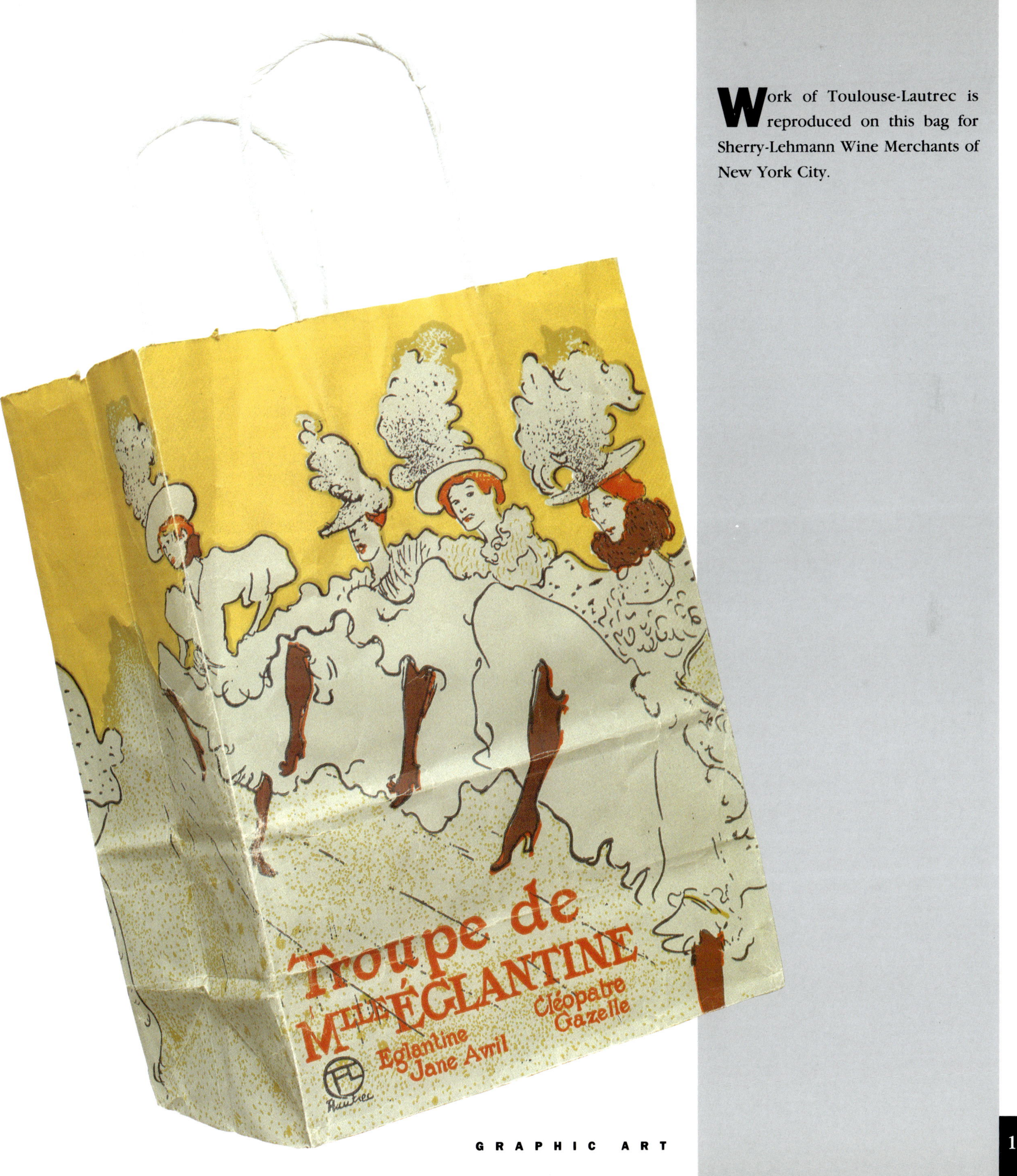

Work of Toulouse-Lautrec is reproduced on this bag for Sherry-Lehmann Wine Merchants of New York City.

Symbolizing the relief brought by the coming of spring to Chicago, the 1983 Marshall Field's spring-promotion bag by Nitti depicts a mystical skyscape with drapes flowing gently in the breeze.

The shopping bag featuring Andy Warhol's soup can is probably the most significant bag in the Smithsonian Institution collection.

Neiman-Marcus is known for its clever and unusual promotions, as this 1981 Christmas shopping bag by Tom Wood of Disney Studios illustrates.

For the British Festival of Minnesota in 1984, Dayton's collaborated once again with the Walker Art Center to produce a shopping bag featuring the work of a famous artist. British artist David Hockney painted a Punch and Judy puppet show for the commemorative bag.

This oil painting by Tom Dawkins reminds us that the shopping bag is more than a utilitarian object, that it can be viewed for its aesthetic qualities (*Lord & Taylor Shopping Bag with Apples and a Pear*).

This contemporary setting at Marshall Field's in Chicago combines Memphis-style furniture with a plastic shopping bag as a home accessory to make an eighties environment (1985).

The shopping bag is part of a life-style created by Horses in 1982 during a Chicago performance-art piece.

Shopping bags may have become status symbols, but this postcard of a Tiffany's window in Manhattan clearly shows that the portable art of shopping bags belongs to everyone.

Imported from Japan by Omnibus, this bright and colorful ceramic shopping bag makes a perfect gift for any avid shopper.

In a whimsical poster designed by Hudson Talbott, the Statue of Liberty is shown exhausted in a cab after a Fifth Avenue shopping spree (*Schlepping Home*, 1982).

PLAIN

BROWN BAGS

In an introductory scene to one of Jackie Gleason's "Honeymooners" episodes from the early 1950s, Alice greeted Ralph as she walked through their tenement door carrying a plain brown shopping bag laden with their weekly supply of groceries. Alice's brown bag, one for strictly utilitarian purposes, was typical of that era. And what more likely color for the bag than its natural brown shade, just as it came from the paper mill? In addition, it was economical. For this reason many stores today still use the plain brown bag.

A variation on the plain brown bag is the addition of a single or multicolored logo. Even a prominent store such as Bloomingdale's in New York created its own clever "Big Brown Bag."

The rustic wood-tone appearance of the brown shopping bag is especially appropriate for certain styles of graphics and some kinds of retail businesses. For merchants who elect traditional or country designs for their bags, the brown background is fitting. Businesses that want to convey a rustic or old-fashioned feeling about them might use brown bags. And what better color of bag for a coffee aficionado's shop?

Yes, the brown shopping bag—which became a household item in the 1930s—will be with us for a long, long time. But it's not so plain any more.

The basic big brown bag finally materialized as a clever creation of Bloomingdale's and has become standard equipment for many New Yorkers.

The muscular logo of the male clothing store Torso, in Chicago, appears in bold black graphics on a brown shopping bag.

For its selection of home fragrances and personal-care products, Crabtree & Evelyn of London chose the brown bag as appropriate to their image.

Associated with grocers and markets, the brown bag was picked for the silk-screen designs of the Summer Farmer's Market in Madison, Wisconsin, in 1985. The design was changed each week for variety.

The African rhinoceros is a fitting choice for the emblem on the brown bag produced for Rhino Playking of Germiston, South Africa.

Whether or not you're planning a safari to Africa, Banana Republic is the place to be outfitted in fashionable safari-wear.

The tropical theme of Bangkok's Neo Scene is depicted on a brown bag with a cut-out handle.

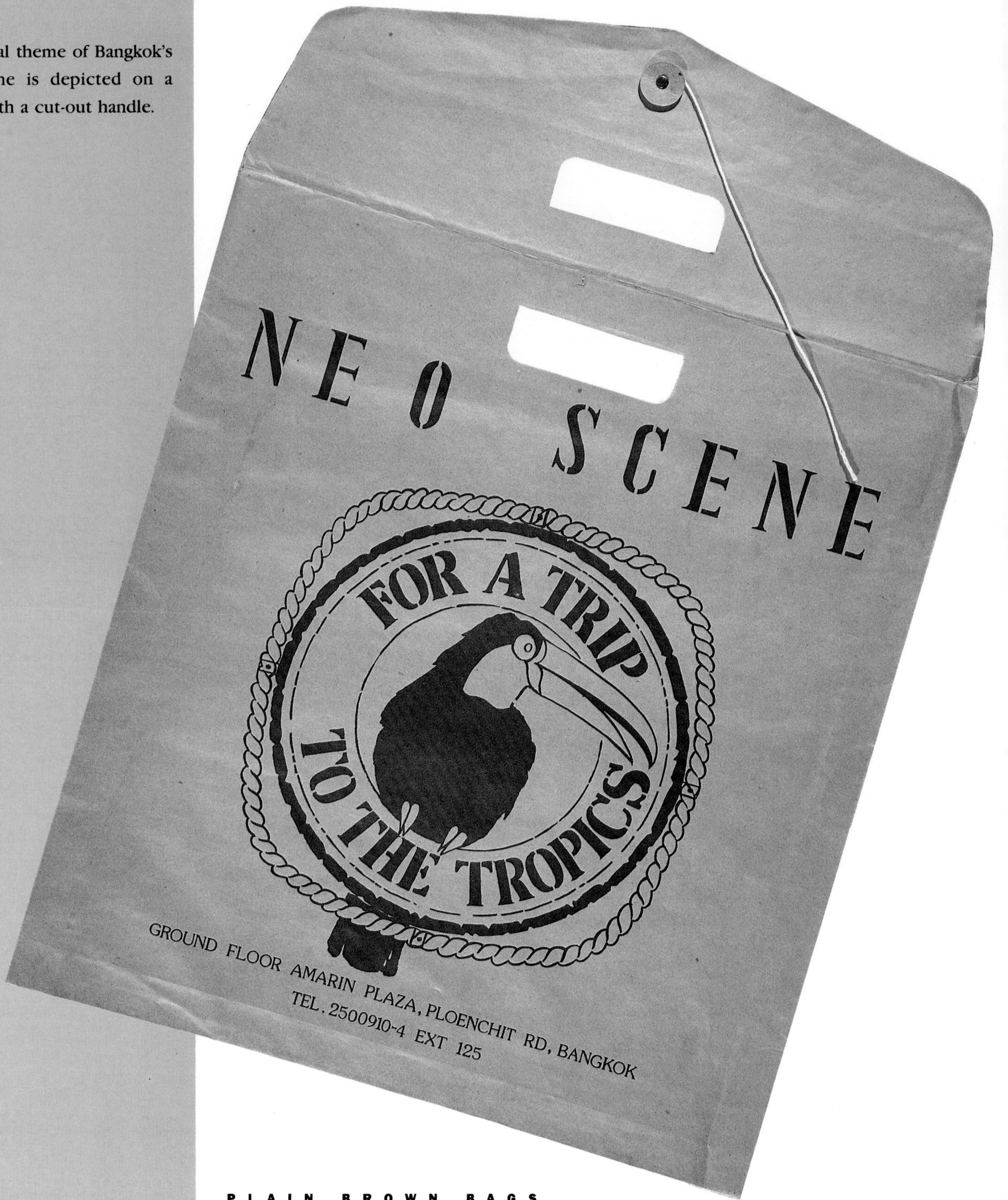

This bag from Germany clearly shows that coffee is appreciated the world over.

Ah! The heavenly scent of coffee," is depicted on the shopping bag of the coffee shop Something's Brewing, in Chicago.

SIGNATURE

BAGS

What do Rolls-Royce automobiles, Gucci handbags, Polo and Izod shirts, Cartier and Rolex watches, Nike running shoes, and Levi and Vanderbilt jeans have in common? Each is generally considered to be among the finest of its kind. And each carries a simple company emblem or signature. Thus, a certain prestige attaches to ownership of these products, because anyone else can easily identify them. Indeed, this identification factor alone has undoubtedly contributed significantly to their success.

An uncomplicated design logo makes a strong statement through its ready recognition. There is sophistication in simplicity. Today, the emblem or signature design found on status merchandise has been adopted for many shopping bags. People like to be seen carrying a bag from Saks Fifth Avenue, Gucci, Bally, Harrods, Polo, and other stores of prominence. The fashionable set in San Franscisco carry Gump's bags. In the Southwestern United States it's Sakowitz.

Of course, there are some practical business reasons for the popularity of emblem and signature bags. They can be more cost effective than many shopping bags, and easier to design. The logos already exist and can readily be transferred to the bags. Few colors are involved. More colors would distract from the focal point of the logos. There is no need to change the designs often. After all, emblems and store color schemes don't change. Besides, changing them would interfere with the identification factor that is the key to the success of emblem and signature bags. An example of this is the famous red-rose design of Lord & Taylor, taken from their early practice of adorning packages with a freshly cut rose.

Sometimes the color of the signature bag becomes just as important as the design. The distinctive red color identifies a Gump's bag at a distance, long before the name can be read. The classy black-and-red glossy texture of a Saks Fifth Avenue bag, or the silver shine of a Bally bag, readily catches the eye. The lavender of New York's Bergdorf Goodman bag is equally distinctive.

Some of these emblem and signature bags have gained such prominence that they have been duplicated in miniature ceramic reproductions which are popular novelty items.

One of the most successful and well-known logos is that of Lord & Taylor. The classic rose and script have stood the test of time.

Using the turquoise color synonymous with its stores, the Tiffany script logo is another easily recognized bag design.

Another classic bag design is Saks Fifth Avenue's simple black and red, with a refined and tailored look.

Gucci's famous red and green stripes appear on this bag as a web belt with a Gucci logo buckle. The background simulates the grain of leather.

With Gump's high reputation as a fine gift store, their name needs merely to appear on the Gump's bag to project their quality and image.

Franco of Bologna uses a design that reminds us of the famous Gucci bags.

The polo player is recognized worldwide as the emblem of Ralph Lauren Polo designs. A simple gold-stamped logo creates an understated, elegant bag.

Small ceramic bags only a few inches high have become popular novelty items. Merchants can order these ceramic bags with their own store logos printed on them, as well as the logos of renowned stores.

PROMOTIONAL

B A G S

It is mid-October in Dallas, 1983. Bright red shopping bags with a cuckoo clock tout the Neiman-Marcus Fortnight, celebrating Germany. The main floor of Neiman-Marcus resembles a German castle, and cuckoo clocks, beer steins, bratwurst, and polka dancing abound throughout the store. Every year at this time, Neiman-Marcus highlights a particular country and transforms its Dallas anchor store into an exciting festival. Window displays, musical entertainment, craft demonstrations, restaurants, and special packaging are part of the elaborately orchestrated celebration. This Neiman-Marcus promotion is an example of how stores become theatrical stages to excite customers and skyrocket sales. Basic to these promotions are specially designed shopping bags.

With "The Odyssey" as the theme for the 1982 Neiman-Marcus Fortnight, highlighted were the cultures of Italy, Greece, and Yugoslavia. The 1981 Fortnight, titled "Orientations," honored the countries of the Orient.

Bloomingdale's in New York annually shows off its theatrics with fall promotions highlighting a country and its merchandise, similar to the Neiman-Marcus fortnights. In the last several years, Bloomingdale's has created dazzling displays to promote merchandise from China, France, Ireland, and Japan.

Marshall Field's in Chicago goes all out with its spring promotion each year, creating a garden of merchandise as the city emerges from its bitterly cold winter. In 1984, Field's burst into spring with bright and bold flowers on its bags, with "Flowering Fields" as the theme.

Houston-based Foley's designed a series of bags distributed in 1981 and 1982 featuring a rainbow of four colors. The colors were changed to reflect each season—winter, spring, summer, and fall. The spring season in Florida inspired a contemporary beach design for Burdines in 1984, entitled "The Best of Everything under the Sunshine."

The opening of the first Bloomingdale's store in the Southwest was a proud event for the city of Dallas. And Bloomingdale's created a bag announcing this was "Like No Other Store in the World."

Store promotions can be used to tie into special events happening in the community. The New Orleans–based Holmes department store organized an Egyptian promotion in conjunction with the "Treasures of Tutankhamen" exhibit at the Museum of Art in 1977 and 1978, with an Egyptian-style shopping bag created for this event.

Department stores are not the only retailers to coordinate major productions. Regional shopping malls put together mall-wide promotions with special advertising, decorations, activities, and displays. Shopping bags featuring the promotion's theme are supplied to all the merchants, and all stores benefit.

Grand openings of regional shopping malls are also occasions for major advertising and promotions. When Dallas's prestigious Galleria Mall opened in 1982, a high-tech bag of color bars on a black background was supplied free of charge to all the merchants. Of seventeen hundred entries, this bag was awarded a bronze medal at the Art Directors' Club of Houston exhibition. Another exciting bag design was created for the reopening of the remodeled Valley View Mall in Dallas.

When mall-wide promotions are created, anniversaries are often used as occasions to celebrate. The Galleria Mall in Houston commemorated its tenth anniversary with a specially designed bag highlighting a multicolored Roman numeral X. This design also appeared on banners throughout the mall and was embedded in the ice of the rink in the central atrium.

Theatrics have become a standard facet of retailing, and major promotions will continue to use imaginative shopping-bag designs to individualize stores and malls. Promotional bags serve as collectible souvenirs to remind shoppers of their experiences at these special events.

With the same design used with different color combinations (opposite page), Foley's in Houston created an exciting series of bags to promote each season (1981 and 1982).

The bold yet simple design of black bamboo shoots on a Chinese-red background expresses the Eastern-world approach to composition for the 1981 Neiman-Marcus "Orientations" Fortnight.

The typeface chosen for Bloomingdale's Irish promotion in New York City captures the rustic charm of Ireland.

For its "New Japan" promotion of 1984 in New York City, Bloomingdale's shopping bag reflected the feel of contemporary Japan, with a modern approach to ancient composition theory.

A bright, colorful bag was designed to commemorate Macy's 1985 celebration of fireworks for the Fourth of July.

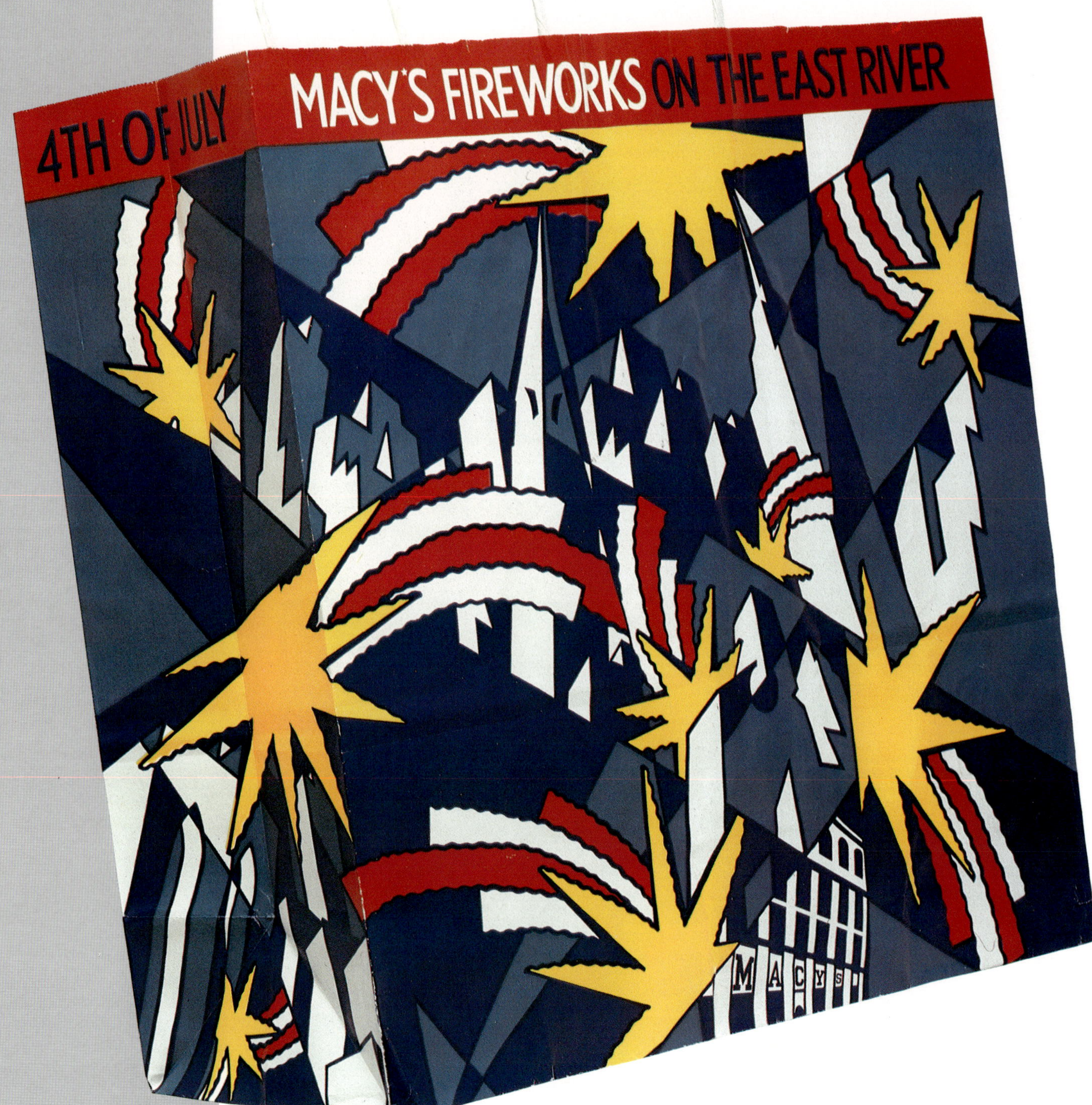

For its 1986 spring promotion, Dayton's of Minneapolis hired the world-renowned Japanese art director Eiko Ishioka to design this shopping bag, produced in conjunction with the Walker Art Center exhibit "Tokyo Form and Spirit" and the spring flower show "Form and Flower."

The unofficial Texas mascot, the armadillo, was featured atop a German cuckoo clock in the Neiman-Marcus German Fortnight, in Dallas, 1983.

The highlighted countries of the Neiman-Marcus 1982 Fortnight, "The Odyssey," are represented by an ancient statue superimposed over a coastal map of the Mediterranean.

In this contemporary bag design for the Galleria Mall in Dallas, the use of texture creates a subtle grid pattern on the black background, noticable at certain angles as light reflects off the surface (1982).

Cactus and the Dallas skyline captured the contemporary Texas spirit on the shopping bags for Bloomingdale's 1983 grand opening in Dallas.

The recognizable symbols of Egypt with the Tutankhamen mask as the focal point, and the familiar colors of ancient Egyptian artwork, make up the Holmes Egyptian-promotion shopping bag (New Orleans, 1977 and 1978).

A modern version of the Roman numeral X uses popular colors from Italy, reminding us of the original ancient Roman Galleria from which the twentieth-century Houston mall was designed (1981).

The Best of Everything under the Sunshine" was depicted in 1984 by Burdines of Florida as a tanned woman with a large pink sun hat under the yellow-sunshine sky.

With "Flowering Fields" as its theme, Marshall Field's took a powerful burst into spring with bright and bold flowers on its shopping bag for spring of 1984.

A profile of a sophisticated woman in pastel fashion colors reflects the quality image of the renovated Valley View Mall in Dallas. Note the "V" logo repeated in the lower background (1982).

CHRISTMAS

BAGS

Like clockwork, the Christmas buying season begins and the new Christmas shopping bags appear. Since Christmas is the biggest shopping season, it follows that the largest number of such shopping bags are manufactured and distributed then.

At the peak of the Christmas buying rush, city streets and shopping malls are scenes of countless bags floating by. It seems that everybody is carrying at least one shopping bag, and some people seem almost engulfed by them.

It is a genuine tradition now. As with the annual appearance of the new lines of automobiles, department stores attempt to outdo one another and even to outdo themselves (over their previous year's design). These bags represent the full range of Christmas spirit. From religious scenes to Santas, from traditional to high tech, from simple design to complex patterns—shopping bags flaunt it all.

Many prominent department stores have their own tradition of creating unusual Christmas bags of fine quality each year. Neiman-Marcus annually uses the cover design from its much-touted Christmas catalog for the design of its Christmas shopping bags.

Another popular tradition is that of Saks Fifth Avenue's December calendar. Each year the month of December can be found on the Saks Christmas bag, with the twenty-fifth highlighted in green against a red background. This bag serves as a countdown of the shopping days left until Christmas arrives.

Other stores create entirely different themes and designs each year. Among notable and attractive bags are those of Marshall Field's. Collections of traditional Christmas items have been featured on several of the Field's Christmas bags. However, in 1984 Marshall Field's planned a sophisticated bag with a gold finish and a fancy white bow. Prior to the actual production of the bag, it was discovered that the gold material would block security sensors that scan customers leaving the store. At the last minute, the original concept had to be scrapped, and the same design in red with a plain white bow was used instead.

All these designs illustrate the exciting artwork inspired by the Christmas season that is created for shopping bags. And at the season's close, one Florida store, Robinson's, couldn't resist designing a bag for its "After Christmas Sale."

These Christmas bags have become easily recognizable as those of Saks Fifth Avenue (1982 and 1983).

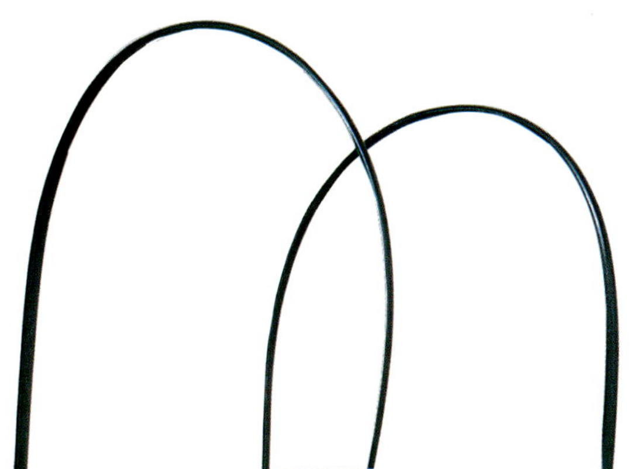

The use of chalk in a highly contemporary style makes this Christmas bag of unusual interest (Chas. A. Stevens, Chicago, 1983).

Masked carolers strolling through an Italian village were created by artist De Paola for the Neiman-Marcus 1982 Christmas bag. Artist Hirschfeld depicts Santa dashing through the snow on this 1983 Neiman-Marcus bag.

Traditional Christmas decorations and gifts represent the Marshall Field's Christmas tradition in Chicago (1982).

An array of German handcrafted nutcrackers create this 1982 Christmas statement for Foley's in Houston.

Bloomingdale's tradition of creative graphics is well exemplified in these two Bloomingdale's Christmas bags, from 1983 and 1984.

Ski slopes and Manhattan skyscrapers make a contemporary Christmas statement for Bloomingdale's in 1985.

The four-color printing process was used here to feature a photograph of a freshly cut Christmas tree carried by warmly dressed models, for Sibley's of Rochester, New York, in 1982.

This was Marshall Field's solution to its production problems with the 1984 Christmas shopping bag.

The Five Senses of Christmas" is vibrantly depicted by I. Magnin as an angel with bright yellow wings and a horn (1983).

After Christmas Sale, Robinson's, Florida, 1982.

COSMETIC BAGS

As a promotional tool, cosmetic and fragrance manufacturers often supply shopping bags to their retailers. And since the cosmetic industry is tied to high fashion, these bags, most important, project image and status. The graphics are highly innovative, attractive, and sophisticated. Though these bags are small in size, they account for an important segment of the shopping-bag industry, and they consistently offer some of the most exciting designs.

The four-color printing process is used to create a strong masculine image for the Antaeus Pour Homme line for men by Chanel.

For Yves Saint Laurent, bold graphics with rich colors and glossy black are used here to produce a sophisticated and contemporary image.

Here, Chanel chose to simply depict its products, matching its colors with drops of nail polish and a stroke of lipstick.

The light contemporary artwork alluding to strokes and smears of makeup create the image for Elizabeth Arden's "Springfevers" line.

Soft pastel flowers treated with embossing and gold stamping produce a chic cosmetic bag for Nina Ricci's "Fleur de Fleurs" line.

Using the four-color printing process. Elizabeth Arden created a sophisticated way to play with color.

G I F T

B A G S

In our contemporary life-style, where convenience and time are highly desired, it is natural that a simpler and quicker method of gift wrapping would become popular. Along with microwaves, fast-food restaurants, and convenience stores, gift bags are a familiar aspect of this contemporary life. The ease and speed of putting a present into a gift bag is often chosen over the more involved method of using wrapping paper, tape, and bows. Just add tissue and a card.

In the mid-seventies, a Dallas-based company, Sample House, came out with a line of small, handled gift bags in bright basic colors. Coordinating tissue paper and gift cards were included in the line. Specialized stores, constantly seeking out new and unusual paper products to offer their customers, found the Sample House collection a perfect addition to their gift-wrap selections. The success of Sample House spurred many manufacturers to include gift bags in their lines.

One exponent of this new concept in gift wrapping, Carolyn T. Young, introduced entire gift-bag ensembles. Each is complete with ribbon, decorations, tissue paper, and gift card, all packaged in cellophane and ready for immediate use. To add a personal designer touch, each of the bags in the Carolyn T. Young line bears her signature.

Further acceptance of the use of gift bags came as Hallmark, the most renowned and successful manufacturer in the social-expression industry, began producing its own gift bags. Hallmark incorporated these bags into its everyday and seasonal gift-wrap lines, constantly adding many new designs.

Many trendy items are now represented on gift bags: Flowers, crayon boxes, musical notes, ice cream cones, and poodles have joined the offerings of solid, striped, dotted, and checked gift bags available.

The basic solid-color gift bag is now available in an assortment of colors and sizes, produced by a multitude of manufacturers. These bags are made by Sample House, The Stephen Lawrence Company, and Equitable Bag.

It's not the size that counts. This little bag printed in Japan by Leadworks adds style to any small token of esteem (4¾″ × 4¾″).

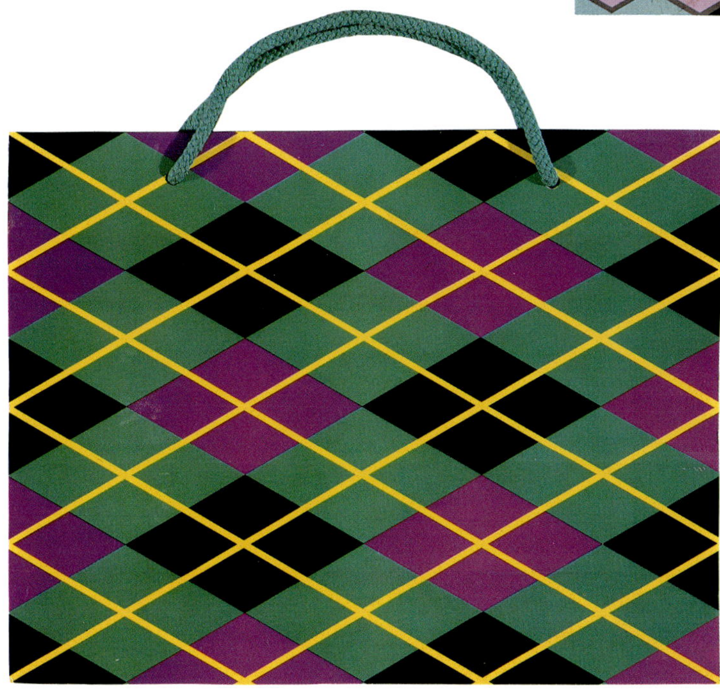

Sharp and bright best describe these two contemporary-design gift bags from The Stephen Lawrence Company.

This "Bag of Tricks" was part of the line of Felix the Cat gifts produced in Japan for Determined Productions, Inc., in 1983.

What better way to give a little Christmas cheer than in this humorous gift bag from Pam Marker.

Whether you are giving a gift for Valentine's Day, a surprise birthday party or to the host of a summer party, Hallmark offers just the right gift bag for your needs.

UNUSUAL USES

The shopping bag is no longer considered to be solely the property of the retail industry. Its high visibility on streets and sidewalks has caused it to be used as an advertising medium for just about any type of business or organization.

If a political candidate needs an army of volunteers serving as walking campaign posters, where does he place his name? Suppose you'd like an unusual kind of exposure for the cover of your magazine, where would you picture it? When the state lottery wants to develop a handbill that lots of people won't throw away, where would the lottery print its message? If banks, airlines, hotels, and other businesses want a reusable and inexpensive advertising gimmick, where do they put their ads? On shopping bags.

In the city of Chicago, where the high population density creates much sidewalk traffic, it is no wonder that the late Mayor Richard Daley chose the shopping bag as one means of campaigning for office. Note that the ecological concerns of the times are reflected in the statement, "This bag is biodegradable," while the credit, "Union made, Local 832, L.B.P.S. & P.W." on the bottom of the bag clearly shows Daley's concern for union labor.

Political shopping bags have come a long way in sophistication since the Daley campaign, as is seen in the two 1984 national political-convention bags. San Francisco's Democratic Convention produced a slick bag featuring scenes from all over the city. The Dallas Republican Convention took a humorous approach, depicting the Republican elephant in western attire riding bareback atop a Texas armadillo.

I wish this was a bag of moolah.

Moolah Instant Lottery

As a means to publicize the opening of the newly constructed Dallas Public Library, this shopping bag was created in 1982 to announce "A New Central Library for Dallas."

In 1984, the United States granted businesses official status in support of the Los Angeles Summer Olympics, and many of these businesses produced shopping bags to tout their status.

Bundles of dollar bills comically drawn were used for the 1984 Illinois State Lottery promotional shopping bag, stating what many state residents carrying the bag might be thinking. "I wish this was a bag of moolah."

World-renowned restaurants have now joined the ranks of businesses offering shopping bags. Whether your eyes were too big for your stomach, or you simply are picking up a take-out order, shopping bags can be carried out from the likes of the popular Hard Rock Cafe in London, the quaint Cafe Du Monde in New Orleans, or the fashionable Russian Tea Room in New York City.

If posh spots are not your style, you could still be seen carrying a shopping bag from a favorite fast-food restaurant—Burger King.

As a natural extension of the grocery bag, grocers have added shopping bags to their stock of sacks. From small produce markets, such as Koepsel's in Baileys Harbor, Wisconsin, to large supermarkets such as an A & P in New Orleans, customers have found this an easier way to carry home their purchases.

Shopping bags are often used to make soft-sell pitches for products. This bag from Japan creates an image of the active life-style of those who own video equipment.

The Metropolitan Museum of Art in New York City is among the many museums around the world to supply shopping bags in their museum shops.

The Italian lighting firm Artemide produced this bag to feature the many angles of the Richard Sapper–designed lamp.

Determined Productions created a numbered limited edition shopping bag to celebrate the thirty-fifth anniversary of the creation of the Charlie Brown comic strip character Snoopy. For the occasion, Snoopy is depicted decked out in a silver and gold tuxedo.

ALL SHAPES AND SIZES

ow small are the smallest shopping bags? Only an inch and a half high. These novelty bags are so small they can be held in the palm of your hand. And an even smaller depiction of shopping bags can be found on a necktie, with the bags being only a fraction of an inch in each dimension.

Of course, shopping-bag manufacturers have developed a number of standard sizes. For instance, the "queen" size measures sixteen by eighteen and a half inches. But many times, the required use of the bag necessitates a specially designed size or shape. The familiar bottle bag evolved this way. Bags of all types can be seen—a cylindrical bag, a cardboard bag, a bag with sculptured handles, a "box" bag with a lid, a bag with a mesh insert, and other such variations.

Fiorucci in New York City is known not only for its bizarre fashions and merchandise, but for its bizarre presentation and packaging. Whether with a clear-plastic drawstring bag featuring a racy woman, a paper shopping bag with a see-through mesh insert, or a self-clamping, plastic-top bag with roses and black dots, Fiorucci always manages to successfully render the element of surprise.

The Dance Centre of London used the standard gusset fold and flat bottom for its shopping bag. But instead of paper, cardboard is used.

By using a drawstring and a side opening, Chicago-based Carson Pirie Scott created a shoulder bag for its 1985 Memorial Day sale. The fish design reflects the fun approach in creating the plastic bag.

This souvenir shopping bag made of Mylar depicts a panorama of the San Francisco skyline from the Golden Gate Bridge.

This vinyl bag is ideal for a day of summer fun at the pool. Sealed with liquid and life rings, this bag is produced by Two's Company, Inc., to be included in its line of vinyl and Plexiglas gift items.

As the availability and price of paper have made plastic bags often more desirable than paper bags, Atomic City in Paris selected plastic for its bold shopping bags.

capp

Within the format of a standard flat bag, die cuts can be used to create handled bags. Halston took the shape of its cologne bottle to create the handle on its men's fragrance bag in 1982. And Capp used the shape from the letter "P" to cleverly engineer a handle for its bag.

The cut-out handle of this La Coste bag forms the neckline of a La Coste knit shirt.

The Asian art of matagiri-paper design has found its way to shopping bags. This beautiful and colorful paper makes for a striking carry-along.

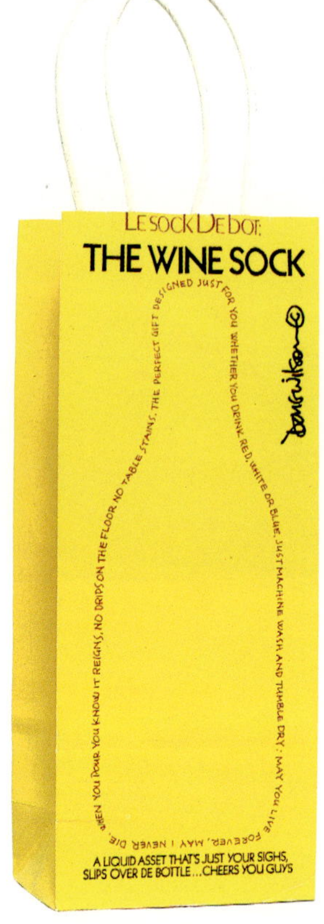

Doug Wilson created "The Wine Sock" for a whimsical means for giving wine as a gift. The bag states, "A liquid asset that's just your sighs, slips over de bottle . . . Cheers you guys."

Harrods of London engineered a shopping bag made of textured foil covered in plastic to carry delicacies from The Food Halls.

Shopping bags seem to appear everywhere, but the fabric of a necktie may seem an unlikely place to find one. Small shopping bags are woven into this tie.

As canvas tote bags are becoming a popular companion, this small canvas bag from Manzanillo, Mexico, proves to be a popular souvenir.

COLLECTIONS AND EXHIBITS

The exciting graphics on shopping bags have inspired many institutions and people to collect these bags. Perhaps the definitive statement on shopping-bag collections is the Smithsonian Institution's touring exhibit, "Portable Graphic Art." This collection has been the most popular of the Smithsonian touring exhibits. "Portable Graphic Art" has toured for four and a half years in two separate sections, with over fifty bookings from Pine Bluff, Arkansas, to Montreal, Canada. The collection premiered in 1978 at the Smithsonian Institution's design branch, the Cooper-Hewitt Museum in Manhattan. Of the hundreds of bags collected by the Cooper-Hewitt, about three hundred and fifty bags were selected to be included in the touring exhibits.

As another example, the *Chicago Sun-Times* put together a major exhibit of over one hundred and seventy bags, which was displayed in 1983. And to applaud excellent technical achievement and printing skill, the Flexographic Technical Association annually accepts entries into competition and presents awards for shopping-bag designs of its member companies.

Collections of shopping bags have been compiled by many people—because they are in the advertising or printing industries, because they are "shopaholics," or because they simply appreciate the artwork on the bags. For whatever reason, bags appear displayed and framed in homes and offices around the world.

The shopping bag truly reflects society's interest in art and graphics. And as our sidewalks have become displays of graphic art, bags have also been taken indoors to receive credibility as an art form through exhibits and collections.

The Smithsonian Institution created a souvenir bag for its traveling shopping-bag exhibit, depicting the shopping bag as portable art with feet.

Some shopping bags in the Smithsonian exhibit were suspended from the ceiling, for a unique means of display.

Brightly colored bags attracted attention among the one hundred and seventy-five shopping bags selected for each of the two Smithsonian traveling exhibits.

In the lobby of the *Chicago Sun-Times* building, shopping bags adorned bulletin boards for the 1983 *Sun-Times* shopping-bag exhibit.

Obtaining a complete series of shopping bags can be a challenge. The animal-skin shopping bags from Abercrombie & Fitch are a favorite series among collectors.

A businessman's satchel made an ideal shopping bag for Hudson's men's department. Unusual concepts like this attract collectors.

This promotional shopping bag was one of the first bags to be printed in the new four-color printing process by Champion International. Note the clear and crisp quality of the photographic reproduction.

Strong graphics and interesting color combinations make this promotional bag from Dayton's of interest to collectors.

With the advent of the four-color printing process, collectors sought out bags with photographic images, such as this 1981 Christmas bag from Dayton's in Minnesota.

A unique use of the four-color process was the dazzling reflections and refractions of light through crystal glass on this Dayton's shopping bag.

Contempo Casuals uses contemporary high-fashion graphics to project its image in the retail fashion industry.

Simple and clean in design, the bag from Paraskevopoulos in Athens prompted a foreign visitor to save the bag as a souvenir of his trip to Greece.

The clear graphics of penguins bearing gifts made an attractive shopping bag for Zootique, the gift store at Chicago's Lincoln Park Zoo. What shopping-bag collector could resist this bag?

Fashion with a Japanese flair makes Parachute a popular store for contemporary clothing. People carrying this bag clearly show they are in step with modern fashion.

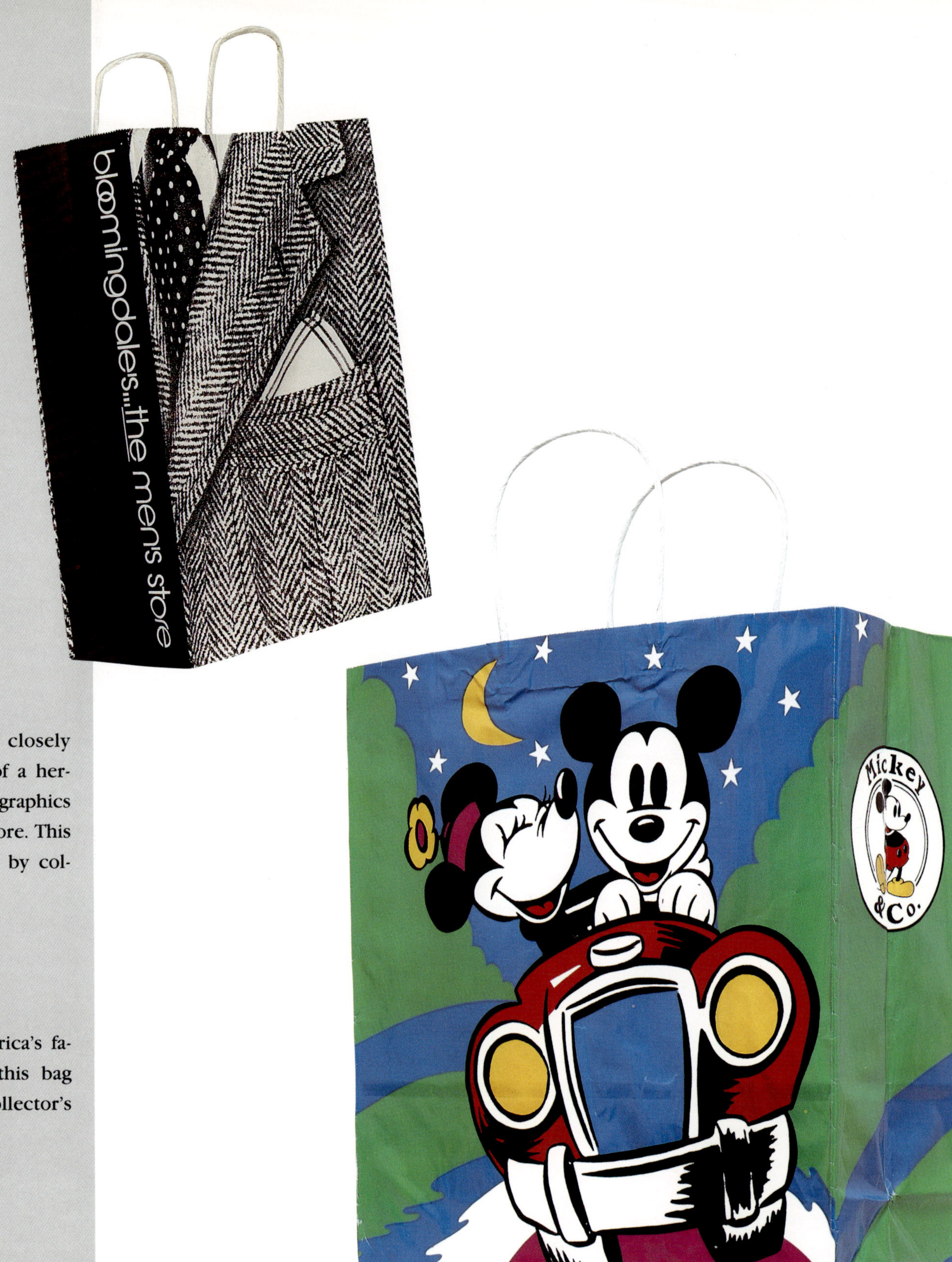

Rich in texture, this closely cropped illustration of a herringbone suit provides the graphics for Bloomingdale's men's store. This bag is considered a classic by collectors.

Bright colors and America's favorite mouse make this bag from Mickey & Co. a collector's favorite.

The contemporary artwork on this Hudson's shopping bag captures well the theme of "A world within a store."

Fiorucci bags appear in most collections, for Fiorucci can always be counted on for the unusual. "Ride 'em cowgirl" might best describe this provocative shopping bag.

The artist for this Italian shopping bag used an airbrush technique to create its unusual graphic effect.

Acknowledgments

We want to express our sincere gratitude to the many people who contributed and assisted in so many ways on this book. Without all their help and encouragement, this project may not have reached completion.

David Aaker
William Albiez
Mark Amenta
Richard Anton
Maria Aulet
Terry Barth
Gerald Berendt
Peter Brooks
John Brunkowski
Jim Butsch
Marshal Butt
McKenna Byrne
Al Calkin
Thomas Campanella
Craig Carberry
Ron Caringi
Glenn Carlson
Dorothy Closen
Larry Closen
Mindy Closen
Stanley Closen
Marilyn Criss
Bob Dachis
Harley Diamond
Steve Dillon
J. D. Doherty
Dennis Dunnigan
Fred Einbinder
Greg Filippone
Norden Gilbert
Jerry Glover
Joseph Golz
Diane Gordon
Margie Green
Judy Guzman
Jerry Haberkorn
Tom Hahr
Celeste Hammond
Dan Hanson
Bill Hellyer
Bill Hershon
Donna Higgins
Ruth Jass
Al Jensen
Cheryl Johnson
Dave Jones
Tom Koneval
Gwen Konigsfeld
Peter Lacher
Ann Lousin
Jess Lozano
Don McBryde
Ken Montgomery
Michael Mulholland
Ralph Nehrenz
John Nowell
Kurt Olsen
Charles Palomino
Greg Parvin
Sergio Perea
Joe Perez
Brad Perino
Dodie Peschong
George Pfoertner
Bruce Poduska
Jim Potocki
Jack Rainbolt
Jeanne Reardon
Robert Reich
Bob Ricard
Brian Richards
George Rishel
Glenn Russell
Roxy Sachs
Margot Sacks
Bruce Sadler
Larry Salvati
Rhona Schultz
Cameron Smith
Gerald Statza
Gene Tankersley
Mark Thackaberry
Jeff Theis
Nell Thomas
Agnes Thulean
Dean Triantifillo
Don Tyree
Rich Urbin
Michael Vittori
Bob Wagner
Marcy Wagner
Ruby Walker
William Webb
Don Weiland
Steve Weiser
Randall Wellons
Ray Western
Mark Wojcik
Ron Wright
David Yates

FARMERS' MARKET '85